Hourglass Museum

Hourglass Museum

Kelli Russell Agodon

WHITE PINE PRESS / BUFFALO, NEW YORK

White Pine Press
P.O. Box 236
Buffalo, New York 14201
www.whitepine.org

Many thanks to the editors of the following journals in which these poems appeared, sometimes in a slightly different form:
Bellingham Review: "Shadowboxing Andy Warhol"
Cascadia Review: "Writing Studio D: A Retrospective" and "In Praise of Staying Married"
Crab Creek Review: "Dune Primrose"
diode: "Periodo Azul"
Her Kind: "Sketch of a Fig Tree"
The Human Journal: "La Magie Noire" and "Taboo Against Mourning"
Mediterranean: "After Leaving the Floating City" and "Slow Swirl at the Edge of the Sea"
Plume: "Darling: An Abstract"
Poet's Market, 2011: "Collaboration: On Some Other Planet We're Newlyweds"

Publication of this book was made possible, in part, by grants from Amazon.com and the National Endowment for the Arts, which believes that a great nation deserves great art; and with public funds from the New York State Council on the Arts, a State Agency.

Cover art: "One Woman Frightened by Max Ernst's Nightingale" by Lynn Skordal. Copyright 2014 by Lynn Skordal. Used by permission of the artist.

First Edition.

ISBN: 978-1-935210-51-1

Library of Congress Control Number: 2013942903

I would like to thank my tribe of writers for their support, friendship, and abundant creativity—

The Theas: Annette Spaulding-Convy, Jennifer Culkin, and Nancy Canyon.

My Kitsap Relations & Writing Group: Jeannine Hall Gailey, Ronda Broatch, Lana Hechtman Ayers, Holly Hughes, Jenifer Lawrence, John Davis, and Janet Knox.

My Across-the-Water Family: Susan Rich, Martha Silano, Nancy Pagh, Elizabeth Austen, and all the Sorrento Booklifters.

The Poets on the Coast: Kelley Henry, Angie Vorhies, and Linda Dove.

RWW Alums & Faculty with a special thank you to Stan Rubin and Judith Kitchen for their continuing support.

Each of you have helped me in the completion of this book and I am truly thankful for your encouragement and your many optimistic toasts.

Many thanks and love to Susie Cramer, Dale & Janice Cramer, Lisa Fritzer, Suzanne Hermanson, Kari Pelaez, Camis, Bill, Hudson, Beckham, & Sailor Davis, Todd Eilert, Deborah Young, Alice Mason, and Rosario Agodon for your ongoing support and love.

Thank you Dennis Maloney, Elaine LaMattina, and White Pine Press for your enduring belief in my work and poetic vision.

Thank you Lynn Skordal for your generosity and the use of your artwork "One Woman Frightened by Max Ernst's Nightingale" for the cover of this book.

Special thanks to the Centrum Artists Residency Program in Port Townsend, Washington, where many of these poems were written and to all the artists, living and dead, who inspired these poems.

Most of all, none of this would be possible without the love, patience, and understanding from my family who has supported me throughout my entire journey as a writer and editor—Rose, who always gives me the time I need and the foods I crave, and Delaney, who inspires me with her own overflowing chalice of creativity and optimistic attitude towards life—I love you both more than I can write. I am truly thankful for your belief in me, as well as your support in all that I do. I can never thank you enough.

And to my mum, Gloria Russell-Baker, for everything you do and have done for me; you are an amazing, wonderful mother and person. I love you.

In memory of my two dads: Gale A. Russell and Bert O. Baker.

for Rose

HOURGLASS MUSEUM

INK AND WATERCOLOR

CURRENT EXHIBITION: HER INVENTED MUSEUM

Reality doesn't impress me. I only believe in intoxication, in ecstasy and when ordinary life shackles me, I escape, one way or another.

—Anaïs Nin

Dear Serious Museum Patrons

The *Exhibition of the Universe* has opened.

We understand meteors and memos
are not uncommon in your life,

but the opening of this exhibit
should not concern your comets or corsets,
your shooting standards, your To Do lithium.

Dear Friends of the Hourglass,
The Guidebook to Escaping, Friends

of the Beetle Wing Blessing and those who live
an Eventful Existence in Turbulent Times.

Dear Friends of the Briefcase,
the Wall Street Darlings in Bowties,

the Buzz Hungry. Dear Friends
of the Doohickey and Thingamajigs,

Friends Suffering with Stendhal Syndrome,
dizzy and fainting from so much art.

Dear Friends of the We-Waited-Four-Years-
For-The-Sequel, Friends who hold Roman candles
and those who sprint to a secure location.

Dear Friends of the Hectic Household,
who took their iPhones camping and found them

covered in dew, For-A-Midlife-Crisis-
Dial-1-800-POEM, Friends with an Art-Saves-

Lives bumpersticker on your Prius
and those who equate watercolor with sadness.

Dear Friends, slapdash or somber, lucky or lucid
dreaming, we want to thank you for holding time's
arrow and setting down your serious schedule

to look up and see the madness
organized in the stars.

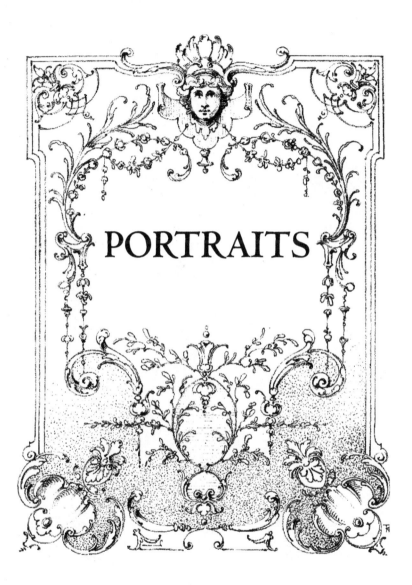

PORTRAITS

The Broken Column

Tell me how you suffer—

in brushstrokes or synonyms,
cigarettes or sickbeds.

The gift shop is selling
small plastic skulls and temporary tattoos
of Frida Kahlo.

I've had enough of the disposable.

I've had enough of pretending I understand
why everything is never enough.

Look at our lives.

We're lost in a web
of logins, in photos
of a friend's family vacation.

I never remember all my passwords.

I never remember when I walk
into a museum, my life shifts.

Earthquake, accident,
layers of God removing the dead
skin from my palms. Frida,
I made a dress from your postcards.

I believe we all love something we don't talk about.

Shattered spine. Fence post leaning against the road.
Illness. How many words are there for pain?

Tell me how the gossip in old books
holds you near,
how whiskey is the valley
you want to visit.

Yes, it hurts to fall—
ache, tenderness
—but each scar is a sign your system is working.

If My Life Were a Canvas,
It Would Be a Jackson Pollock Paint-By-Number

I Blue:

Imagine this: you're spread across the page
of a dream and it's morning. There was a storm
last night and the robin's eggs have scattered
across the lawn.   Some broken, some not.

2 Yellow:

The sink is always full
of disappointment.
Unnoticed daylight,
a measure of sadness—
chipped sunflower plates
overpowering the perfect
blue delphinium teacups.

3 Black:

Sometimes the crows remind us, we are only ink
and paper. Puzzles to solve, silver
to seek, and when the light dims, holes appear
against the universe, in tubes of paint
gathered from the barn—
something will be stolen
from someone else's nest.

4 White

Book of ghosts.
Whispers and watermarks.
Whatever still reflects: paper,
waves, a dove suggesting God.

5 Orange

A crowd of drunken lovers. Newspaper
hats, new couples falling from couches and love-
seats—the pleasure remembered,
never the regret.

A Moment Ago, Everything Was Beautiful

It's been a long time since I couldn't open a jar of mayo, you said.

In your world, this meant the universe collapsed
and the stars had become crumbcake.

Satellites shattered, flour sacks spilled,
and we were a pastry mess in the kitchen.

In the past, we were small heroes.

Now we search the web for online assistants,
new tools for things we could once do.

We shouldn't judge our lives.

We shouldn't judge our lives
by what we can't
twist or hold onto. I heard the sky

that morning was the color of bruises, a blossoming
meteor, a crumpled tail of a comet sprayed
against the crosswalk.

But we missed it all. Inside,

we were considering a life of unopened jars.
So many things we kept shut.

If I think back, I'd believe we went hungry
that day, hungry while the planet slingshot itself
into another galaxy and heaven moved a little

closer. Dark matter angels mingled over oceans
and bubbling cities filled with unopened jars,
all we had were cupboards and cupboards
of challenges.

You said, *Sometimes I still want to be needed,*

so I let our kitchen become a flood
of time and you, the only thing keeping me
from going under.

Slow Swirl at the Edge of the Sea

Listen, love—the cliffs are tired
of restraining us, tired of the questions
we ask each other about time. But
we've forgotten our schedules tonight
and find luxury in the silk pillow-
case, camisole, the petal wings of moths
fluttering at the window. We lie
together in a bed of beach music
above a small village of fishermen,
of ferries and pathways.
When they lower the boats, the sea
swallows hard and we slip beneath a blue
brushstroke, not knowing who will stay under
and who will make it back to shore.

Portrait of a Couple on a Cliff
After Twenty Years Together

After a night of tiredness, of a too-tight corset,
I deserted the party, that part of the atom, particles
of light.

I craved the casual, wanted to be the woman
in worn jeans and t-shirt, dropping my ball-
gown over the Golden Gate Bridge.

Tell me, how long have I been your splinter,
your social gravestone, your mistress
of distraction?

You are Bastille Day
while I am a drought in Zanzibar.

You are the complex Allegory (of Riches) of California
while I am a wallpaper border of napping cats.

Love, how many times have I stenciled forgiveness
in your bathwater, brought you apricots
after an evening of suck.

I can't relate to your razzle-dazzle, your wish
for voluptuous when my symphony is spanx.

Dear One, you chose me because of my love
for handkerchiefs, tarot, for antique spines.

My younger self was so much more mermaid,
so much more collarbone, not a museum
of lackluster, an echoing clock ticking:

bedtime, bedtime, bedtime. Cut me
some slack, or love me because I'm slack,

my fingerprints smudge your history,
the beehive evenings where we once buzzed.

Remember rose-velvet couches, nightingales
escaping their paintings, and hazy geography
full of cliffs to fall from.

I know there are steep exits all around us
and sometimes we slip with only a branch
of a hemlock to hold us up.

Fortune Telling Parrot

To be the master of your own fate means sometimes
         you have to rip up the instruction manual.
Sometimes it's a Bible. Sometimes it's a drawing of success.

The parrot said, *Travel.* The parrot said, *Flight.*

It described my life as a rollercoaster, though I prefer
         bunny hills and kiddie-cars, and I've tried to stop
asking parrots and carnivals to solve my problems.

The parrot told me all emergency exits lead to museums.

The parrot found my pocketwatch, told me to be happy
         for what I have. *Stop trying to be responsible*
for everyone. The parrot squawked, *Read spontaneously.*

What the parrot really wanted was to be held.

And maybe that's what we all want—to know the theme parks
         in our minds are really just a hall of mirrors.
Sometimes we have to determine our own emergency.

When we ride the rollercoaster while in love,
we become the breeze.

Souvenir Boxes

If you think you are the mermaid, think again.
You are the ocean holding the mermaid afloat,
trying to change the world a dolphin at a time.

Even if it hurts, watch the sunrise.
Pico de gallo, pico de gallo. Salida del sol.

Bora Bora
= *amazing.*

We're so busy we forget
we're out of wine. Irony.
Headsnapper. Mad House-
wife. Raised by Wolves.

At first there were
whitecaps. Now?
Not enough water
to draw a bath.

Understand, it's never been easy to live
when we're trying to escape ourselves.

I'm in a fever of doubt, so
you suggest I find my fan
club, wave from a balcony,
lower every expectation.

Maybe I'm still the mermaid.
Maybe the ocean is your hand.

I went to a psychic and her parrot
said, *You will eat the wild strawberries*
on the dunes, then fall asleep. I assumed

this meant a good life;
we were so hungry then.

I remember when our sea
of bathwater spilled onto
the bathmat, you spoke
to me in only washcloth:
backbone, backbone, breast.

Never enough,
said the parrot.

I am trying my best
to be your cocktail,
your emergency exit,
your whimsical kite.

Imagination is an echo chamber,
the parrot kept repeating.

Never mind
sometimes
we are lost.

Self Portrait with Escape Ladder

Even in this blue year, colors
I swear I am still in search of
overwhelm me. Some people know
the sapphire oar, the cornsilk sail, the aqua
art in the middle of this ocean
sky. Maybe the painting is an entrance,
an unlocked cage, a church. Maybe
I don't own the word blue
I would rather apologize later,
find a doorway now.

Portrait of the Artist as a Young Traveler

Because I love the less fortunate,
      blues fill my luggage like the blouse

I left on the bedroom floor; I forget
      what's needed. The sound of a suitcase

zipping around absentmindedness,
      the challenge of life is making everything

fit. For everyone who never smiled in school
      photos, for all who've wandered city streets

not knowing where they were
      or feeling alone, I've packed kindness.

My suitcase spills over
      with constricting bras, but they're coming

with me. Like angels incorrectly measured
      for wings, our shoulders ache

from all we carry. The ticket's been purchased, though
      the destination is heartache. Purgatory opens

and a tavern full of saxophonists tries to lure me in. Voodoo
      books. Strawberry ale. Dixieland jazz. The foam

in the glass spills over onto my hand. And in the back,
      a dartboard with someone's beating heart

as the bullseye—the matadors retreat
      as I arrive and quickly remove their spears.

Line Forms Here

I. Open on Mondays

In the middle of my museum—
and by that I mean, my life
—there is loss.

Sometimes I nap
through the saxophone solo,

sometimes my body curves
around the notes like a bird
trying to protect her nest
and by nest I mean, art.

I'm longing for something I cannot name.

Your time spills
into my writing.

My bookshelf overflows
with future commitments,
dates with strangers I'll never meet
in person.

Memory replays the past—
our lives spent walking the dog, the other
dog, the dead dog we still talk about.

Now, it's hard to stay up past ten.
I'm a jazz performer who's misplaced her song.

The voice in my head tells me to count

my blessings.

Why does tenderness make me uncomfortable?
Why do I talk about the things I cannot change?

II. Flash Photography Prohibited

I place *solitude* in a frame on my desk
and call it, *The one I love.*

I am cutting acquaintances from my life
without written apologies. I'm burning
bridges to keep the crazy ones
from following me home.

Maybe if we were something special. . .

No, there are people I cannot live without,
people who make bracelets
out of clay beads and burn the toast.

I try to give them my time.
I try to give them my right,
so they don't have what's left.

It's a game of balance where the mousetrap
rarely catches the mouse.
It's not about loss, but about freedom.

. . .if only we were in some useful occupation.

It's knowing the saxophone solo
comes eventually, and understanding
museums and families are struggling.

I'm longing for a few people
to love me up close.

At night when my prayers turn
to wishes, I ask the constellations:
Protect me from what I want.

After You Tell Me You Want to Build a Diorama of Your Grandmother's Suicide

After three glasses of wine, we talk about boxes,
wooden barn boxes, feather and egg, lock and key
boxes, poetic theaters, and we lose our place

—there are too many Josephs in the world.

I tell you, *Joseph Campbell built boxes* and you ask,
Myths to Live By? The Masks of God?

No, not the follow-your-bliss guy,
but another Joseph. This Joe builds boxes
to charm us.

All night we google Josephs on my iPhone—
Conrad, Cotten, Prince—all night and sea
salt chocolate mousse, garlic shrimp, a salad shaped
like a waterlily. I trust blue cheese, candied pecans.

After three glasses of wine, we have lost art
and now find photos of nooses, of Joan Crawford,
Whatever Happened to Baby Jane, cock and balls
at VooDoo Donuts.

We are googling our conversation
to create a virtual shadowbox—a video of a baby
panda sneezing, misspelled tattoos, John Cusack
holding a boombox, and Conan O'Brien.

Between Con-Air and bacon-wrapped dates,
you mention you went to school with Nicolas Cage

—*Nicolas Coppola,* you say and we set aside art
and speak of the vineyards in Napa Valley.

You tell me, *We covered our teacher's car in pages*
from James Joyce. We are not Dubliners,

but women who delight in forgetting
the topic—*Cockatoo and Corks, Dime-Store Alchemy,*
Hotel Eden, Penny Arcade Portrait of Lauren Bacall.

Joseph Cornell, we have found you,
shimmering near the glassybaby, collecting objects
at our table, and what was once yours becomes ours.

Frida Kahlo Tattoo

I wear a temporary tattoo
of Frida Kahlo believing
I can change the world

and if not the world,
then a lightbulb, the channel,
change the binoculars from blurry
to focused gaze.

I'm walking through a museum
wishing I were someone
else, trying to determine

if inspiration is taught
or a god-given gift.
Either way, I'm tired.

Frida and a stranger take notes
on my insecurities,
Frida and the museum guard,
Frida and the exit sign.

I don't believe we should carry backup
plans in life's suitcase—

they're too easy to unpack
like living a life in yoga pants,
so comfortable our hips spread
into new timezones,
apathy becomes less rare.

Frida is tired of my mindtalk,
my head-in-the-oven, finger-on-bake
attitude. How many hours have I lost
because I wasn't paying attention?

She tells me to quiet, as if she won't
rub off soon, as if I can survive
without having her near my skin.

How To Make a Picasso Cocktail

The passionate people confront her.
It's after midnight and the artists fall
forward, fall onto the balcony with arms open.

She's mixing drinks, serving mini quiches
to party guests who say: *Give me*
a museum and I'll fill it.

Cognac. Red Dubonnet. Lime
juice. Five teaspoons of sugar, one
is optional. Sugar is always optional.

She shakes vigorously, chills
herself as Picasso pounds at the backdoor—
she's deciding whether or not to unlock it.

The passionate people serve her
well. Well drinks with the hope
Salvador Dali will drop in.

It is after midnight and she is thankful
for the sweet and seductive.

Lucky when she can be more than one,
when she can be the artist and the cocktail,

be the mini quiche in a world
of biggie fries, biggie drink.

The passionate people never forget
when they create, they save themselves—
a heart attack becomes an almost heart attack.

Take me, I am the drug.
Some days she almost dies from an overdose

of satisfaction. She pours sugar on her life
and drinks the artist's marrow
in the bone of her glass and she lives.

Drowning Girl: A Waterlogged Ars Poetica

I don't care! I'd rather sink—than call Brad for help!
from a Roy Lichtenstein painting

As I go under, I wonder if there's a reason for art?
For poems and taffeta dresses I haven't worn in years.

I don't have time to fall inward
or to spend the day obsessing
about how I haven't written anything
of substance.

I'm floating in the sea, watching killjoys,
I mean, *killdeer*, run across my shore.

Call it lack. Call it stuck in the muck
of creative debauchery.

There's no dessert in the picnic basket,
so I swallow time. My mouth is full
of hands and numbers. I ask for seconds.

I eat from everyone's plates, drink enough
of the red sea to take me under.

I am gluttony with a wristwatch,
hectic in my need to get what I can.

The killjoy sings:
Enjoy yourself, it's later than you think.

I dream of typewriters, marble
sculptures—all things that sink.

Cormorants dive like falling ampersands,
killdeer become small commas in the sand.

Nightingales fly from closets
of clouds, from white taffeta dresses
hanging from sky.

I have to make a choice:
reach for them or let them pass.

Self Portrait with Reader

To create is not enough.

We must live with our hearts
in our hands—like Mary.

We must hold the blood-
red heart and not be disappointed
when others look away.

This is the simplest way
to say yes. To say, *I am here*

giving you what I'm afraid
will scare you, yet I am
holding it in my palms.

Disappear if you have to.

Disappear into the cracks
of the world and call it
an earthquake. Fear shakes

itself on us and we decide
how much we can take.

Reader, I want to tell you
the hearts we hold will continue
beating even after we leave here.

Be the statue on the dashboard
traveling hopefully,

even if what you hold
drips onto the floorboard, even
if you have no idea where to go.

SKETCHBOOK
OF NUDES

in the middle of predicting my life

I asked about joy and you gave me
your wound

> *wasp in a wine glass*
> *lost chalice and planet sickness*
> *pocketwatch left on a grave*

you said   *sometimes we have expectations*
you said   *sometimes you have impossible expectations*

then our lives resembled cognac

> two years in oak
> bitter orange   vanilla

I asked if this would all work out

Yes
you said as if you were lying

but time and God and the seasons have got to be
on our side

most of us connect through pain

this is what you said
when I was searching

for my swansong
for my keys

for my life to mean more than meringue
      or a paycheck
      or a clean kitchen

we're designing a language of sidesteps
turning off
the radio   the television   the news

show me the escape route for artists

I want to know the words for waltzes
we never danced

miss guided
lackadaisical as career choice

we can't remove ourselves from the syllables

but we can be the sunshadow on the hardwood
hipswaying our way across the room

I wonder if I might be lonelier
if I didn't have loneliness

      this is the riddle the poet asks
      when there are no poems to write

the poet continues questioning after the bottle
is empty

after the audience has gone home

if the trophy on the mantel
has meaning

what do the oversights represent

or simply

can you address the empty chairs and not regret
the silence

when you finish speaking and nobody applauds

in the corner of the painting called success
the signature is blurred

I hang my life
on the wall to understand
why I'm here

I asked my crowd to catch me

I said   *your world was too mainstream*
            so I made my own

I became an emperor moth fluttering
on Leonardo da Vinci's to do list

> *Get hold of a skull*
> *Nutmeg*
> *Describe the tongue of the woodpecker*
>   *and the jaw of the crocodile*
> *Get your books on anatomy bound*

if only I could get my bills paid
if only the rain would stop

sometimes when I sleep
my dreams mean more to me
than my life does

what am I forgetting

anxiety exists
at midnight

the haunted armoire
calls to me

tells me
    there's medicine I didn't take
    a pet I've neglected to feed

at night madness is the bedspread
I pull around me

what did I forget
who is going to die

most winters I make a container for my soul
and what appears to be an escape route
becomes a box

I didn't mean to become the spent meteor
all those sparks alarm me

all those winters
this was who I was

even as lightning struck the pond I worried
the fish would swim out of sequence
scatter in their duckweed-covered home

most winters I try to rescue everything
in my life though I stay underwater

keep the pills in the cabinet
surrender to my imagined storms

I don't want to be absorbed
by the chaos

but things are beautiful
because of the chaos

I lollygag in the afternoon
woolgathering
knowing I won't sleep well

    I never sleep well

at night when the fog drops
like a blanket on my neighborhood
I am homesick

the moon is just another kind of clock

I fall through the calendar pages
like falling out of bed
falling through paper days

    we are the stories we tell ourselves

biography is not destiny
but sometimes
everything needs to be rewritten

you may remember how I'm always discussing
what's broken

      the artists and what shatters
      wristwatch   pocketwatch
      wine glasses and the wasps we tried to catch

but sometimes I see the world as flawless

      everything is perfect
      a moment ago, everything was perfect

though it's hard to carry the handbook I wrote
about living intentionally

the pages are always falling from it
and I'm always revising
because I never get it right

in the room of language
above my desk and notebooks

there's a canvas with a moon
sketched inside my lover's mind

each night he asks

> *how can we kiss if we have paper*
> *over our faces*

in the shower the water
forms letters on the tiles

    I decided to start anew
    to strip away what I had been taught

no one believed me when I said
a poem dripped down my shoulder blades

mirror beetle became *miracle beetle*
the rescued became *the rescuer*

I found kismet in the bodywash

congratulationsandgoodluck
dripping together as one word

either way things were changing

sometimes I trust so much

    should I

either way it's a slippery world
though sometimes we find a chalice
in mirrors made of steam

I'm attracted to the residue of imagination

> *instead of risk   say fortune*
> *instead of view   say float*

every morning birdsong
every morning
and I stay inside

> *what people want to do most in life*
> *they avoid*

a messenger
sparrow appears with happy news
at my window

it weaves letters into its nest

GOD EXISTS

after a spring of hard rain
the letters begin to fall

GOD EXI TS

the *S* becomes a snake beneath the tree

this is how I feel each winter
this is how I always feel in winter

make beautiful things

he says this
when I'm cranky

in the middle of predicting my life
I realized the future isn't what it used to be

don't worry
everything's going to be Bora Bora

       I stick a bandaid to my heart
       to keep the joy
       from bleeding out

       I make corpse revivers
       for friends who stayed too late

at the end of the day we can endure
much more than we think we can

       this is what my tattoo said before
       it vanished

       this is what Frida says
       each time she visits in my dreams

INK AND
WATERCOLOR

Sketchbook with an Undercurrent of Grief

I escape disaster by writing a poem with a joke in it:
The past, present, and future walk into a bar—it was tense.
There's everything to kill with laughter. I browsed
the magazines in his hospital room. At my father's
last breath, I saw an ad for sky.

My father always said he was part Irish, part Scotch.
I used to jog, but the ice kept falling out of my glass.
I think of Warhol's Dom Pérignon ad—dead artists
returning to sell champagne.

My father's body was moved from the room,
they put ice on his eyes—the only organ healthy
enough to donate. Did I start out by saying:
I escape disaster by writing a poem with a joke in it?
Those last five words weren't necessary.

A girl walks into a bard.

La Magie Noire

I.
Sometimes darkness
is the beauty I am made of—

it's January and I've locked the doors,
I'm refusing to answer the phone.

Sometimes when I'm absent
of Vitamin D, the staircase murmurs:
Jump.

Sorry, the life you ordered
is temporarily out of stock.

Most winters it's easier to hibernate,
clean the windows
in my mind. Imagination:

taking madness and giving it
a loving home.

II.
I have always wanted to attend a party
where someone wears a lampshade,
where a woman slips
into a coatroom with a stranger.

But these are not my parties.

Mine have schedules, cloth napkins,
side salads. Someone mentions The Son of Man.

Someone mentions thread count.

I have an uneasy relationship
with inspiration. I wear black boots,
dance the hubbub alone in the bathroom.

In a conversation about behavior,
I thought she said, *You must be popcorn.*
But what she said was, *You must be proper.*

Another side salad, please. Another
glass of wine.

III.
In the closet, my skeleton
reconnects itself.

How long has it been since my aunt woke up
as part of the universe?

All the French artists believe in night.

She once told me there were many definitions
of crazy,

then passed me a voodoo doll of myself,
a bullseye in the shape of a human heart.

My aunt would have said, *Be more
popcorn.*

My aunt would have said, *All the best artists*
believe in night.

Understand we are all trying
to create something.

Did I mention the light was touching everything?
Did I mention her voice was in the clouds?

Periodo Azul

Because the dress was worn.
Or wasn't.

A blue of forgetting.
A blue dress I might fold
in a basket and carry to the meadow.

The weathervane cannot tell me
if it will snow.

The blue isn't
mine, but I wear it. Through

frost and foolishness,
a field of mourning,

a Sunday morning when I awoke
to learn you were
no longer. Blue

dress of basket. Blue dress
of memory, hospital parking lot,
missing bead in my bracelet.

Because I was worn,
I slept in the car, maybe

the blue dress was a blanket, maybe
a pillow. I was a hollow-boned

bird in the meadow, blue wings
of my dress. Maybe a god of blue,

a lullaby of willow.

How far can I run from myself?
How can I remove everything
from my skin and still be warm?

I raise the dress over my head,
it becomes my sky.

Taboo Against Mourning
for Susan

Once in a museum, the crystal
from your father's watch disappeared—

we had been reading poems
and the clear face of time broke away.

Beside us—ghosts of artists shattering,
an exhibit titled: *Séance: The Only Way to Live.*

If life is loss and future is what we hold onto,
let's hang our memoirs

on the laundry line outside our childhood
home where the day was a sundial and we were lost

in the overwhelming scent of lavender,
in the rosemary bush that wouldn't stop

growing. We have starlight and cliff swallows,
we have house of sea and house of sky.

For years we've washed our paper dresses,
our paper suits. How many times will we write

about loss, about *then* and *when* and the songs
of tick tick ticking? Poems leave

our fingertips and the planchette calls back
the ones we love. Little plank, little heart,

little to remember as time moves on, still
we are a tribe of women who hold their fathers'

watches, who watch them break and fall
and sometimes, we misplace time.

Poems shift through the day: talking
boards, mystic hands. Sometimes

I consider how we disappear
in the numbers of a pocketwatch.

We light two candles and what we hold—
two dazzling flames we refuse to let burn out.

Untitled (Composition in Blue)

We learn self-reliance and to hear the voice of God, too. . .
—Beauford Delaney

I don't really blame the weather
for being beautiful
when I wanted rain,

but blame myself
for being distracted by sky.

I blame myself sometimes

for not being beautiful
enough, not starlet, but wanting
to be how excess words are beautiful
—lapis, cornflower, denim—beautiful,
but unneeded.

Maybe we're what remains.

An untitled painting is a wish. Blue
iris, blue collar, blue
Monday and yonder.

Blue bike on a blue trail,
cement and the crack
of my wrist, my head hitting
the pavement—blue blood
turns red when the oxygen
arrives—

I didn't think

of beauty, but maybe
I should have.

That day I became a canvas of red
paint, red skin, untitled
in a bike helmet—scarlet and flame,
crimson and ruby.

On Li's couch I saw a fog,
but didn't call it heaven;
I called it heaving,

of not having enough
water and becoming my own
dehydrated life. Aftercrash.

Somewhere between purgatory
and not trying hard enough.

I don't blame the sky
for making me leave my house
or the bruise on my arm, my leg,
the slight bump on my cheek where
I butterfly-kissed the pavement,

so much prettier
than saying I was graveled-down,
devil-licked.

But this is what I think
when I write how God is not a man
in a white robe, but a deity in a blue

housecoat, blue jeans. She wears
the blue faint sky.

I was taught to think I must exist
on my own, but in photographs
I am always posing

with another.
Sometimes I'm happier when I lose
the word *faith*
and replace it with *blue*.

Like the kite that caught up to the sky,
painted with clouds, I lost track of it,
but it was connected

by string, something I was holding,
something I could always
bring back.

Directions for Collecting and Preserving Humans

Because I cried, facedown
on the table,

my acupuncturist said,
Lungs hold grief, while the heart
holds joy.

You're not heartbroken,
but lungheavy,
all those clouds inside you
        ripping you apart.

I almost understood
how wisps of lungs
could sew themselves
back together

as she pinned me, repinned me
again, but instead I said,

What I expected to be easy
was a series of shadows, butterflies
without their wings.

She said, *Once there was a "you"*
in euphoria, but we don't live there,
we don't live in that box anymore.

After Leaving the Floating City

In Italy, I understood to be happy
I shouldn't regret
I spent our rent money
on a painting
of the moon in my lover's mind.

That summer we navigated Venice
with a map of broken statues.
We pointed to the corners
of buildings we thought no one noticed,
collisions of saint and sky.

I understood my life
was already falling into place
like a history of what to do
found in the notes of philosophers. I studied
the patterns of women in the piazzas

and asked myself,
which shadow glittered, which shadow
dimmed? I learned not to regret
the little things that changed me—
the wilted flower in the gondolier's shirt,
the dove that refused my bread.

Daringly Balanced: The Life of an Artist

I. View

Ask the artists who lean
over balconies if lilacs circle
where they dwell and they may
agree: *much of life is about loss.*

II. Risk

Sometimes pennies are the only pieces
on our gameboards
and everyone wants to read the poem
we're afraid to write.

How To Be a Genius in Many Different Fields

Ask embarrassing questions

Trust that life in despair is much more
interesting than life in perfection

Fear everything from ocean liners
to grasshoppers

Adore luxury, weakness, and old age

Realize if you want angels, you have to stand in line
with demons

Know there's beauty in the words you leave out

Rediscover the confessional poets
and their poems about love and love and
each other

Know the more you admire yourself, the more
you'll become a catastrophe

Fortunately. . .or unfortunately

What is useless is sacred

Ask what a rhinoceros horn
has do to with anything

Understand every artist has the right
to defend her work

Distant Horizons: An Abstract

I

Early morning and I find beauty
in imperfection. Rain. Fog.

Too tired to sleep, I become a wanderlust
in cardboard shoes.

2

Success: its usefulness is overrated.

3

A friend comes over with a Ouija board.
It spells out: *Bourbon. Where's the band?*

Just because you're dead, doesn't mean you can't
have fun.

4

Poem: a form of negotiation for what haunts us.

5

There's a ghost in my home,
but we've named her Tilde
as punctuation can't hurt us.

6

Sometimes I slip on the wet chattermarks
during a long walk where I'm lost
in my head and I find myself
pleasurably disoriented.

This happens in poetry too.

7

Keep the faith and trust in so far as possible.

8

When the wind pushes clouds
out of the sky's solo, I realize I'm spellbound
watching the evergreens in my yard
lean backwards, a jazz quartet.

9

We learn how not to break, but bend gently.

Sketch of a Fig Tree

Halfway through the day with the sun like a halo
over my neighbor's house, I think about God
and time and if it's possible to feed my soul with a pen
and ink drawing I saw at a museum by an artist
whose name I didn't recognize.

Somewhere across the country my house is falling apart,
or maybe it did years ago, returning to my old neighborhood
to realize the streets were never as big as I thought
and the house I lived in was not as nice
as the house down the road, but I was never allowed
to walk that far.

I'm older now and what's falling apart is the sunset
I try to watch from my office window
where I'm surrounded by books
and it doesn't matter how much the fog moves in
or if there's a neighborhood where kids fight

about the color of poppies. I think back to the fig tree
that grew in my yard and how the leaves always reminded me
of being somewhere else or in the middle of a Rousseau painting
where the jungle was a prayer and everything I needed
was above me and all I had to do was reach up,
all I had to do was open my hands.

Meaningless Consequence
life on paper, unlimited edition

To suffer together is to suffer
with beauty, the white shirt
of glistening black ink, the fortune

of a wet print worn across a heart-
beating chest. This is what we have
—words letterpressed to our bodies.

To suffer beautifully is still to suffer

on a bench, an unseen fog in the cracks
and wings of the owl flying to the end
of the sea. Sometimes we follow

the glint of rosebuds through the light
of wine, our glasses unsure of why
we have loss. We drink what we have left.

CURRENT
EXHIBITION:
HER INVENTED
MUSEUM

Luxury, Calm, and Desire

> *Do not postpone joy.*
> —Teo Ruiz

She spent the summer drinking
pomegranate martinis, praising the bees
that sipped from her glass.

Who's to say what's a weed, what's a wildflower?

Lilac books, aster stars, tulip cafés—
there's a buzz in knowing those who create
might be a little safe.

Dune Primrose

She carries brushes
    and bone,
skulls and stones

wrapped tightly
in a towel.

She will carve a cross
    from soap,
float

a small tombstone
in her bath.

There's a painting
    she thinks of
while she bathes,

Black Cross,
New Mexico—

opposite of the white
    soap she moves
across her breasts.

Her town is a room
without light.

She opens the window
    and the scent
of the desert disturbs her.

When she trusts
a painting enough

to bathe with it,
    the canvas wrinkles
like her skin.

But this does not
return her

to her hometown,
    to her history
buried with each

dead aunt, each name
carved in stone.

She places her hands
    between her thighs.
Her bath

is a cold grave. She thinks
she's the ground

women rest in, but
    she's the small leaves
sprouting from their palms.

Death of a Housewife, Oil on Linen

In the beginning, there were chores
without names and morning
flowers expanding into a sunrise.

There were months
without leaving the bedroom,
windows full of streaks and sheets

too large to fold. No,
there was not enough time
for champagne, for matching

bookends in the library, or even sweeping
the dog-fur, those sad clouds,
down the stairs. There were only ticks

of the clock, the silence
of the Brillo pad asking her to dance
the watusi when what she wanted

was to tango with another or a key
to unlock the front door and waltz
herself into another life.

Mural of a Writing Residency
or The Best Part about Manet's
"Dead Matador" is the Bull

The family you left
at home is playing some card game
you could never get the hang of,

while you count the minutes
before you have to shower, before
you return to your regular life.

You are not the mother in the blender
ad, the one who combines mango,
banana, and strawberries to make her

family a creamy, healthy treat.
You feel the blade and not the smoothie.
You are the blender and not the woman

pressing the switch. Sometimes
you want a life of different rooms
you can walk into—now

you are a writer, now mother, now
lover, now a stranger sleeps in your bed
and she is you. There's some sort of card

game you'll never get the hang of, call it
life or *motherhood*, call it trying to understand
you were never meant for middle

management, how you resent your employees
and having to show up on time.
You sound spoiled here. An artist who wants

to live in her obsessions unlike that friend
who said, *I'm so glad you finally took*
that vagina out of the living room,

when referring to your painting by Georgia O'Keeffe.
You still aren't sure what to hang
above the sofa—*The Dead Matador?*

Picasso's *Gertrude Stein?* You know you lost
a part of yourself when you had to explain
to a new acquaintance

that people still publish poetry
books—*You mean, right now? You mean,*
there are poets living in America and not just Spain?

Yes, you said holding your wounds
because the blood was flowing from your chest,
ready to burst into her eyes,

and you didn't want to blind your new friend
because she's unaware that what you do
actually exists. *But how do you get paid?* In the sigh

of satellite images, you see your writing shed
in a bullfighting arena and sometimes
you hide out there, not writing, just pretending

you're not home, from people who need
the backstory, people who hold the spears. I hope
you're paid in quiet time. I hope you're paid

in sandpipers and Barbie shoes you find
on the beach. I hope you're paid in never learning
how exactly to play that card game, but to watch

as if you care. The blender is not a gadget
in the advertisement, but the life you create.
There's a moment when you return home

after a week of writing to realize you still love
your pets and the people who exist in the space
next to you. You still hold your heart

when people ask about poetry, but only because
you know it's beating. Like the bull
searching for its *querencia*, you leave and return

to the same spot, not that it will save you, maybe
it makes you more predictable, or maybe
it makes you twice as strong.

Portrait of an Argument

oil on canvas, 20' x 50'

There's his and hers and theirs and ours.
And the neighbor's. Never forget
the neighbor and his cat
that sits on the fence between our home
and hisses.

I'm currently between sides at the moment, somewhere
over the hill and underwhelmed.

Somewhere between the grass is always greener
and I just need to water my own grass.

We are breaking plates and calling it
a celebration. We are calling it love
with a capital O.

I am somewhere between throwing a mango
at the wall and imagining I am on a sitcom.

I'm the not the door slamming but the one
who wakes up at 6 a.m. to watch the clouds
pass by the window.

For two hours.
For two hours of heartbreak.

I am on the side
of the sky, on the side of the clouds
and their quiet disagreement with the sun.

Woman Under Glass

from the Exhibition of the Modern American Mother

The woman wants to be the woman her family thought
she should be, but she doesn't like cooking. She doesn't
like cooking or other mothers or doing crafts. In fact,
she hates scrapbooking. She fucking hates scrapbooking.

The woman who wants to be the woman other people
want her to be doesn't say fuck. She doesn't say fuck,
or piss, or shit, or fuck. She understands words feed
and poison her. Continually and at the same time.

The woman who wants to be the woman she could be
is inconvenienced by field trips and volunteering.
She thinks teachers should do their own filing. She thinks
there is a version of history with her name on it. A banner.

An award. What she does is feel resentful about pancakes
in the shape of Mickey Mouse. She knows Disney must have
hated mothers, must have hated every mother because
they all die in his movies. The woman who wants to be

the woman she wants to be loves her family. She knows
she doesn't tell them enough, knows she's running past
the breakfast table with a pen in her mouth and this
is not normal. Normal mothers make breakfast

and aren't trying to write poems that question
the consequences of art and creativity. The woman
who wants to be the woman who is remembered
and not reminded of what she is not, is trying her best

even though it looks as if she is failing or falling or doing
a pretty good job or better than most. She is unsure
about her rank as mother or who is judging. She can hear
a few of the women in her family singing from the closets.

Or crying. She isn't sure. She decides not to care
about ghosts or plans or cleaning windows or stereotypical
roles based on gender. She thinks this is easier to do
in her head. She sweeps and thinks. And thinks. This is her

downfall. This is how so many hands have themselves
wrapped around her neck, her waist. This is how
she's been waltzed into too many messy ballrooms,
so dizzy from spinning, she blames no one but herself

for not believing she knew the steps, but for seeing
the sunrise through the curtains in the window
and never believing there could be light.

Writing Studio D: A Retrospective in Spring

Imagine this: it's the day before Easter
      and beautiful if you love sun

and birdsong and egg hunts, but not
      if you're wishing for rain, if you think Jesus

is a distraction from real life and birdsong
      is the unexpected alarm now waking you

before 6 a.m. But it is, beautiful, the day before
      Easter and you have to drive forty-five minutes

to watch your daughter at a two-minute Easter egg
      hunt, but that is three hours from now

and right now, you're in a room typing a poem.
      Imagine this: It's the week before Easter

and you've planned a writing retreat with friends
      in a haunted apartment to write

for five full days, five full days, because there is
      nothing more you want to do

than lose yourself in your words. But you've
      learned to stop saying "retreat" and use

the term "residency" because others
      think you're on vacation, some sort of

girls' weekend with wine and pedicures. No,
      this is where they've become confused.

This is where a friend says, *It's so nice*
        your husband can watch your daughter,

as if he's not related to her, as if he's not
        responsible for her care. And

this week I found myself
        annoyed because my daughter's teacher

wrote me after my husband went
        on a field trip with her class:

Your husband was a wonderful chaperone.
        Thank you for sharing

him with us. And I wanted to hit
        reply and say, *Dads get points*

just for showing up. Imagine
        the teacher ever writing

my husband to say, *Thanks for sharing*
        your wife with us. Thank you

for not only being a dad who showed up,
        but also a Filipino dad,

you've added so much diversity
        to this busload of white kids.

Imagine this: It's the day before
        Easter and I'm beautiful

and not bitter that my generation is still
        stuck between women who live

for their men and the girls who expect
        more. Maybe they will resent

their husbands for caring too much
        about hairstyles, for using product.

There's an Easter egg hunt in less than
        three hours and I'm frothing

about relationships, about already having drunk
        my first cup of coffee and it's empty,

instead of realizing I'm still here, in this
        room looking out to a forest

of blackberry bramble, of trees with moss
        on the north side, just like

in the Camp Fire Girls book I had as a child
        when I believed that good deeds

created beads and patches, and I could rename
        myself Kekoa because it meant

Brave One, because I would grow up
        to be thankful for my ability to start

fires when the other girls fumbled with their flint.
        And while in this town, Jesus is a distraction

because he's walking up the street in a tiny toga
      with an Elvis in wings

singing, *Hunka-hunka burning love* during the Easter
      parade because it's hippie-dippie here.

I know where I reside best and how I can leave
      last minute from a beautiful day-before-

Easter-morning to arrive back into my life of family
      members who forget to drag the garbage

down to the corner and be thankful I only start fires
      because someone needs warmth

but otherwise, I can leave the flint in my pocket and
      no longer create spark just to prove I'm the best.

The Art of Forgiveness

She carried a speech
in her pocket, rehearsed
simplicity, *We need to talk,*
again and again.

But when he arrived late
with a bouquet of wildflowers,
she poured them over their canvas
even though he went inside for a vase.

He had no idea
who Jackson Pollock was,
but he loved how she could cover up
the years with petals
of poppies, how chaos
became charming, dripping in paint.

Menacing Gods: An Abstract

Madness is a meaningful way to exist.

Sometimes it's hard to know
who we are, our attention's lost
before the centerfold is unfolded.

Sometimes plans are missing.

The future is a paper airplane
hitting me in the face.

It never lands softly.

Sometimes we don't know
if the article we want to read
has already been torn out.

The litter we fill our calendars with.

Madness is another way
to come unfolded. Future sins
are my favorite—

let's lose the map, find our red shoes.

My spirit is tangled. Hold my hand,
darling, let us stroll into hell.

Red Poppy

Forever a lover, I kept you
in the vestibule of my heart, the inner
hall where women in red
danced through all four rooms.

Forever a lover, I kept you close
because I could, because you cherished
my curtains, the white fence I built
around you.

Today in the atrium, the foyer
of my heart, I served you
chamomile tea for your anxiety,
rice crackers to calm your nerves.

There are hornets
in your veins, but still I want you
close, your muddy shoes
in my hallway, your forgetfulness

throughout our home.
When it comes to leaving,
doors open. You return
with flowers, unlock

our world and set it on the table,
overlooking winter, winter
chores and the palpitation
of water pipes.

Red poppies in a blue vase
blooming in my body.
December spigots unwrapped,
exposed to the cold

and everything is frozen, then
not. Two lovers in the corner
and all we didn't expect overflowing
around us, always rushing in.

In Praise of Staying Married

In perfect middleness,
in the winter of waxwings
and imperfect feathers, lost

friends—
we are not leaving
our nest. Like others

who aren't entwined
in the honeysuckle, in the blackberry
vines, we stay knotted.

Like clouds refusing to be part
of the mushroom, we rained.
We loved our curves

and our appetite
for showers. Don't get me wrong,
our mistakes have flooded

the valley, flooded
our blue farmhouse until
the living room was underwater.

Praise the trees and chairs
we climbed to stay dry,
not the wings

that might have brought us here,
but the round bellies
of birds hopping through

puddles, not beautiful,
but full, complete
with their berry-stained beaks.

Shadowboxing Andy Warhol

Andy Warhol speaks to me in voodoo
lilies, organic crackers, and gingko leaves.

As I undress, I am the hourglass
corset over love, under chandelier music
from the crystal ceiling.

Andy worries that it's raining
celebrities

while I arrange the language
of portraits, the pocketwatch and paper
garter of life. I rip up my mini-
dictionary,

buy us society sunglasses—
*Keep your mirrors shiny. Always
let the valet park the car.*

Andy tells me not to settle—
we should have assistance when assistance
is available, find our best kiss

for a luxurious life, better
than the satisfactory breakfast
of nothing or none or no one.

Andy speaks to me through soup cans
and mismatched Marilyns:
Be exotic, but don't be grandiose.

I think we are lost

on a series of bridges and I complain
how my life has too many options,
too many roads to choose,

but he hushes me
—don't let your spirit be tangled—

I thought we were adrift,
but we were always on track.

Collaboration: On Some Other Planet We're Newlyweds

You asked for sizzle, but it was late
and all I could give you was mumble.

You asked for sizzle and I gave you
myself as a fossil, dunes when you wanted waves.

In Jupiter years, we've been married
a couplet, eighteen months, in a world

of purgatory that equals one grain of sand. If that.
If that and the oversized plates

we thought we needed, the Blue Danube pattern
of our shadows as we walked from the mall.

Now two calicos later, two calicos and a little less
sizzle, we chant our desires to ourselves

as we brush our teeth—
A little more, you say. *A little more Jupiter.*

A little more Frida Kahlo and The Love Embrace
of the Universe. This and in the background,

someone made of clouds is holding us.
I rub your shoulder blades

trying not to alienate, our alien nation
of household, the pop and sizzle of starshine,

so many photo albums melting together, yet
in a different galaxy we might be young.

Surrealist Angel

Be lost.

Be the howling stars or the quiet
coyote. Arrive at the roadway
without a plan, without knowing
where you will go.

Turn left.

Be the firefly. Be the moth.

Be the couple in the car who has fallen
in love for the hundredth time.

Be their clock, their hands.

Be the bell chiming from the church
and the patrons leaving
the bar. Be the drink they keep
in their hands, the holy water
they bathed in.

Turn back. Turn forward.

Be the headlights of the taxi,
the sidewalk, the dark stairs
leading to a bright apartment.

See the glow in the window
and want to be that glow.
See one person reaching for another.

Be the silhouette behind the shade.

Sky Cathedral Ghazal

Her invented museum was a hopeful arboretum full
of paper blossoms, overflowering fragments of papercuts, full

of sharpening in need of pencils, godsends
and pillows spilling from the bed. It was not a beautiful

disaster of strangers who had nothing
in common, but a diary of friends, full

from brie, from chitchat and the red wine
they drank in clay chalices filled

to the edge of a cliffswallow night. It sounds beautiful,
golden, but sometimes the birdsong was full

of sorrow. Sometimes the shatter was the eggs
when the mud nests didn't hold. She could be too careful;

she worried about being an imitation of herself—
self portrait with dictionary, an awful

moonflower, Mary-Tyler-Moore-often-than-not.
Could she be a plagiary of earlier work, a full

jigsaw puzzle where she jammed pieces
together? Maybe. She was writing though, filling

her hearth, an inglenook of unexplored language. And this
was all she wanted—a god on her side, untroubled, fulfilled.

Darling: An Abstract

All night I've been typing you
a letter,

looking for language
in the canvas of another, in Sylvia Plath's
tulips, in Georgia O'Keeffe's bones.

I hear about their sadness,
how history began in an orchard.

·

All night we drank sangria and a small apology
equaled so many truths,

the fine wine of traveling
landscapes through open-mouthed guests
who wanted to be somewhere else.

·

This box is only temporary.

This box is full
of cards and for the last two nights, I chose
the Hanged Man.

I wasn't surprised when I found myself
crying in an alleyway with laundry,
clothespins. Time was a nightshirt
then, a blue onesie.

Sometimes the gods tell me
I don't go far enough.

•

When you ask about my life, you add
commas to your voice.

I, too, can pause.

I wrote to you because I was lonely
and only know my side of the story.

•

I think about Chagall and moons and flying,
but enough on trying to understand harmony.

My dedicated satellite.

•

The envelope tastes like longing.
The hourglass museum remains unfinished.

•

In the simplest way, we are all becoming the light.

After Hours Dining at the Hourglass Café:

Welcome to the Cafe

Hourglass Museum

Appetizers:

HONEYCOMB:

Entrees:

QUINOA SALAD WITH MANGO:

MENU

Drinks:

MAD NEWTON MARTINI:

Desserts:

BASKET OF FIGS:

THANK YOU FOR DINING   AT THE HOURGLASS CAFE

Notes:

Many of the poems in this book were inspired by artwork listed below. Most can be found very easily online through your favorite internet search-engine.

PORTRAITS:

DEAR SERIOUS MUSEUM PATRONS: "Stendhal Syndrome" (also called "hyperkulturemia" or "Florence Syndrome") is a physical condition that may include dizziness, fainting, quick heartbeat, confusion, and sometimes even hallucinations when a person is exposed to too much art (or a large piece of beautiful art) in one particular space or in a too-short period of time. The term "time's arrow" is a concept developed by British astronomer Arthur Eddington that suggests time's "one-way direction" or "asymmetry."

THE BROKEN COLUMN is after the 1944 painting by Frida Kahlo of the same name.

A MOMENT AGO, EVERYTHING WAS BEAUTIFUL is after a museum installation by Gary Baseman of the same name.

SLOW SWIRL AT THE EDGE OF THE SEA is after the 1944 painting by Mark Rothko of the same name.

PORTRAIT OF A COUPLE ON A CLIFF AFTER TWENTY YEARS TOGETHER: "Allegory (or Riches) of California" refers to the 1931 mural by Diego Riviera of the same name.

FORTUNE TELLING PARROT is after a music box artwork by Joseph Cornell of the same name circa 1937-1938.

SOUVENIR BOXES was inspired by the shadowboxes of Joseph Cornell and incorporates Cornell's interpretation of "the imagination as a metaphorical 'echo chamber.'"

Line Forms Here is inspired by the 1964 collage and ink on paper "Is That the Height of Your Ambition Johnny?" by Joe Brainard and Frank O'Hara. The lines, *Maybe if we were something special* and *if only we were in some useful occupation* were borrowed from the artwork and modified slightly. The end quote, *Protect me from what I want*, is by Jenny Holzer from her 1983-85 "Survival" series.

After You Tell Me You Want to Build a Diorama of Your Grandmother's Suicide is for Annette Spaulding-Convy and includes references to Joseph Cornell's artwork as well as what we had for dinner that night.

How To Make a Picasso Cocktail: *Give me a museum and I'll fill it* is a quote from Pablo Picasso. *Take me, I am the drug,* is a quote from Salvador Dali.

The recipe for the drink is as follows—
Fill a cocktail shaker with ice cubes. Add all ingredients.
1 1/2 oz. Cognac
1/2 oz. Red Dubonnet
1/2 oz. fresh lime juice
1 tsp. sugar (5 dashes – 1 is optional)
Shake and strain into a chilled glass. Garnish with orange peel.

Drowning Girl: A Waterlogged Ars Poetica is after the 1963 painting by Roy Lichtenstein of the same name.

Self Portrait with Reader: This poem was inspired by a pho-toem (a digitally collaged photograph and poem) created by Nance Van Winckel entitled "To Travel Hopefully."

SKETCHBOOK OF NUDES:

In the middle of predicting my life: The full quote is *The great thing about making cognac is that it teaches you above all to wait. Man proposes, but time and God and the seasons have to be on your side* by Jean Monnet.

IN THE CORNER OF THE PAINTING OF SUCCESS: Leonardo da Vinci's "To Do" list is from the artist's anatomical notebooks and personal papers, which were written in approximately 1510.

SOMETIMES WHEN I SLEEP: In 2012, I donated the "haunted armoire" to an auction to support a local environmental nonprofit organization; however, I still find myself dreaming about it even though it is no longer in my home.

IN THE ROOM OF LANGUAGE was inspired by "The Lovers" (1928) and "The Thought Which Sees" (1965), two paintings by René Magritte.

IN THE SHOWER THE WATER: The quote in this poem, *I decided to start anew, to strip away what I had been taught,* is by Georgia O'Keeffe.

MAKE BEAUTIFUL THINGS: The quote, *At the end of the day we can endure much more than we think we can,* has been attributed to Frida Kahlo.

INK AND WATERCOLOR:

LA MAGIE NOIRE is after the 1945 painting of the same name by René Magritte.

PERIODO AZUL: The title of this poem comes from Pablo Picasso's "Blue Period" and is dedicated to my father, Gale A. Russell, who died in September 1992.

TABOO AGAINST MOURNING is dedicated to Susan Rich and was inspired by events and exhibitions from our "Taboo Against Beauty" reading with Allen Braden and Oliver de la Paz at the Frye Art Museum in 2010.

UNTITLED (COMPOSITION IN BLUE) is after the 1961 Beauford Delaney painting of the same name. This poem is for Lisa Fritzer who cared for me after a mountain biking accident in May of 2010.

DIRECTIONS FOR COLLECTING AND PRESERVING HUMANS was inspired by the book, *Directions for Collecting and Preserving Insects* by C.V. Riley, which was published in 1892.

DARINGLY BALANCED is after the 1930 painting by Paul Klee.

HOW TO BE A GENIUS IN MANY DIFFERENT FIELDS was inspired by quotes and interviews from Salvador Dali.

DISTANT HORIZONS is after the 1952 Beauford Delaney painting of the same name and includes two quotes by the artist, *Keep the faith and trust in so far as possible* and *We learn how not to break, but bend gently.*

SKETCH OF A FIG TREE was inspired by Henri Rousseau's 1910 painting, "The Dream."

CURRENT EXHIBITION: HER INVENTED MUSEUM:

LUXURY, CALM, AND DESIRE is after the 1904 painting "Luxe, Calme, et Volupte'" by Henri Matisse.

DUNE PRIMROSE was inspired by the 1929 Georgia O'Keeffe painting "Black Cross, New Mexico."

DEATH OF A HOUSEWIFE, OIL ON LINEN is after the 2007 painting by Lola Scarpitta of the same name.

MURAL OF A WRITING RESIDENCY OR THE BEST PART ABOUT MANET'S "DEAD MATADOR" IS THE BULL: This poem refers to the painting

"The Dead Matador" by Édouard Manet as well as the portrait "Gertrude Stein" by Pablo Picasso. The word "querencia" is the Spanish word for the place in a bullfighting arena that the bull returns to. Some believe it makes the bull predictable and more easily killed, while others believe it's the place the bull becomes defensive and finds its strength.

WOMAN UNDER GLASS is after the 1985 painting by Martina Hoffman of the same name.

WRITING STUDIO D: A RETROSPECTIVE was inspired by and dedicated to the Centrum Artists Residency Program in Port Townsend, Washington, where many of these poems were written.

RED POPPY is after the 1927 painting by Georgia O'Keeffe of the same name.

IN PRAISE OF STAYING MARRIED is dedicated to Rosendo Agodon.

SHADOWBOXING ANDY WARHOL was inspired by the "Andy Warhol Media Works" exhibit at the Seattle Art Museum in 2010.

COLLABORATION: ON SOME OTHER PLANET WE'RE NEWLYWEDS is dedicated to Rosendo Agodon.

SURREALIST ANGEL IS after the 1983 sculpture by Salvador Dali of the same name.

SKY CATHEDRAL GHAZAL is after the 1958 sculpture "Sky Cathedral" by Louise Nevelson.

AFTER HOURS DINING AT THE HOURGLASS CAFÉ contains links to four extra poems, which can be accessed through these web addresses:

www.agodon.com/hourglassappetizers.html
www.agodon.com/hourglassentrees.html
www.agodon.com/hourglassdrinks.html
www.agodon.com/hourglassdesserts.html

Thank you for visiting the Hourglass Museum.

Kelli Russell Agodon is a prize-winning poet, writer, and editor from the Northwest. She is the author of *Letters from the Emily Dickinson Room* (White Pine Press, 2010), Winner of the ForeWord Magazine Book of the Year Prize in Poetry and a Finalist for the Washington State Book Award. She is also the author of *Small Knots* (2004) and the chapbook, *Geography* (2003). She co-edited the first eBook anthology of contemporary women's poetry, *Fire On Her Tongue* and recently completed *The Daily Poet*, a book of poetry writing exercises she coauthored with Martha Silano.

Kelli is the co-founder of Two Sylvias Press and the editor of Seattle's literary journal, *Crab Creek Review*. She is an avid mountain biker, paddleboarder, and kayaker. She never underestimates the power of museums and good dessert to heal what ails.

She writes about living and writing creatively on her blog, Book of Kells at: www.ofkells.blogspot.com

Visit her at www.agodon.com

or on Facebook at www.facebook.com/agodon

Author photo by Susan Rich.

In Kelli Russell Agodon's third collection of poems, *Hourglass Museum*, the yearning to create is what moves us forward. Through car rides with Andy Warhol, temporary tattoos of Frida Kahlo, and long dinners with Joseph Cornell, we walk hand-in-hand through a paper museum where what inspires intersects with our regular lives.

Hourglass Museum offers a dazzling selection of poems inspired by artwork and artists that explores personal relationships and the struggle (emotionally, financially, and spiritually) of living a creative life. Agodon understands the importance of how art influences our lives and how we balance delicately realizing that we only have so much time to live and create. *Hourglass Museum* is a meditation in beauty, tenderness, and knowledge reaching far beyond most poetry that's being written today.

"There are just handful of contemporary American poets whom I do not want to live without, whose books I keep by my desk and never lend out. Kelli Russell Agodon is one of these poets. *Hourglass Museum* is such a beautiful collection. Lyrical, intelligent, magical and honest, the poems are both of this world and out of this world. Her uniquely true and mystical voice is like a glass of pure water: refreshing, healing, and oh, so necessary."

—Nin Andrews

"Kelli Russell Agodon's *Hourglass Museum* is a carefully planned leap into the unknown. Her poems are an intense vision of the power of art to heal, to help us understand ourselves and our world. There is much striving in this powerful, engaging book: to make connections, to succeed, to love well. Agodon invokes artists as disparate as Kahlo and Cornell, Picasso and Pollock, as a way into the world she creates for us in her deft and musical poems. She brilliantly succeeds at helping us to look up and see the madness/organized in the stars."

—Wyn Cooper

"The poems in *Hourglass Museum* may be triggered by visual art and artists, but they read as Kelli Russell Agodon's very personal struggle with making poetry and living with the consequences— artistic, social, emotional. It's an intelligently conceived and moving collection, and the greatest pleasure of all is the line-by-line revelation of the poems, which are always lively, witty (even when they are sad), surprising, musical, addictive. Reading these poems is a joy."

—Kathleen Flenniken

Printed in the USA
CPSIA information can be obtained
at www.ICGtesting.com
LVHW041255200124
769142LV00003B/85